THE APES OF EDEN

THE AGE OF THINKERS

The Apes of Eden
The Age of Thinkers

Jon P. Gunn

Chula Vista, CA

The Apes of Eden – The Age of Thinkers by Jon P. Gunn
Copyright © 2015 Kent F. Gunn

All rights reserved. Except as permitted under the U.S. Copyright Act of 1976, no part of this publication may be reproduced, distributed, or transmitted in any form or by any means, or stored in a database or retrieval system, without the prior written permission of the publisher.

This book is a work of fiction. Names, characters, places, and incidents are the product of the author's imagination or are used fictitiously. Any resemblance to actual events, locales, or persons, living or dead, is coincidental.

Published by iCrew Digital Publishing
Website: icrewdigitalpublishing.com
eMail: icrewdigital@gmail.com
First Print Edition: February 2015

Paperback ISBN: 978-0-9864449-1-3
eBook ISBN: 978-0-9864449-0-6

Cover Illustration by Annie Hobbs
anniehobbsillustration.com
Formatted for Createspace by Sebastian Certik
blackseahorsepress.com
Special thanks go to Jim Bennett (jim-bennett.ca) for his wonderful reviews and editing assistance.

iCrew Digital Publishing is an independent publisher of digital works. We support the efforts of authors who wish to self-publish in the digital world.

Apes of Eden on the Internet

Website for The Apes of Eden: apesofeden.com
Facebook Page: facebook.com/apesofeden
Follow @apesofeden on Twitter

CONTENTS

I.	Harpies and Heretics	1
II.	The Philosophical Enterprise	9
III.	MS=More of Same	16
IV.	PhD=Piled High and Deep	22
V.	An Essay on Morals	32
VI.	An Essay on Morals (Concluded)	39
VII.	The Gift of Prophesy	48
VIII.	The Deluge	52
IX.	The Reformation	56
X.	The Mystics	62

HARPIES AND HERETICS

That brings my record past the Hero Age
and into one of Scholar, Scribe and Sage—
a sort of "passing phase in evolution."
Thinkers found no permanent solution
to the questions Eden's Tribe pursued,
and wrought no basic change of attitude.
It was an aberration, as you 'll see,
in Eden's long-term tribal history.

   As we had wandered over hill and plain
our Faith had undergone tremendous strain.
In all the lands our questing Tribe had trod
no race except our own believed in God.
And once we stopped, and had some time to think,
new questions rose, which pushed us to the brink
of Skepticism. Eden's first great Sage
who led us from our homeland (in an age
long buried in antiquity by then)
had made his main appeal to tribal yen
for Novelty. Since then, much time had passed;
and now we found his word was not the last
as far as evidence and logic went.
Though Eden's bounty might be Heaven-sent,
the same could not be said of lands we'd long
become aware were built completely wrong—
nor of the world at large. We could have thought
of ninety ways it might be better wrought.

   Without the sun, nocturnal winds were chill.
They made us shiver by our fires, until
the sun arose at dawn to warm the air—

2 ♦ The Apes of Eden: The Age of Thinkers

then, all too soon, became a scorching glare
that hammered on our heads and shoulders, and
rebounded from the glowing, smoking sand.
All day we longed for evening cool, but then
confronted night's remorseless cold again.

   It wasn't hard to think of better ways
to plan the cycles of the nights and days.
It would, for instance, be a real boon
if sunshine went through phases, like the moon,
so that its full intensity would roast
our hides one week of every month, at most.
Or else, if days were just a fourth as long,
the sun would not have time to wax so strong.

   An even better way it could be done
would be to tilt the axis of the sun;
had it around the Earth's horizon gone,
we'd always be enjoying dusk or dawn.
With neither noonday heat nor night's cold breeze,
we wouldn't alternately scorch and freeze.

   Again, we knew that God created land
to give terrestrials a place to stand;
but what could He have had in mind when He
created it in endless quantity?
This vast expanse was clearly not designed
with those who went in search of God in mind;
it separated us from distant goals,
and bruised our feet, and overwhelmed our souls.

   And other qualities the cosmos had
—although we couldn't call them good or bad—
were inexplicable, as if designed
expressly to confuse the mortal mind.
For instance, shells are grown in lakes and seas,
and yet we scribes can find them where we please.
Whole epics, scratched on strings of shells, describe
the triumphs and misfortunes of the Tribe.

The plains are strewn with shells, and in the hills
they're found by handsful in the arid ghylls.
But how could shells have come from sea to land?
Such oddities were hard to understand.
If God had wanted desert lands like these
producing shells, He should have made them seas.
Some said there had been seas here, long before;
but this was speculation, nothing more.

    Nor had our long-enduring faith been crowned
with much success—since God remained unfound.
Was this the way a Quest for God was meant
to be—or were we just incompetent?
Or was it possible that God preferred
His privacy, as some of us inferred?
In other words, was Satan's lying tale
true after all, that we were doomed to fail?

    These burning questions and a hundred more
were undermining our esprit-de-corps.
My records never mention apes who went
completely atheistic; but we spent
another thousand years in hot dispute
of philosophic issues deep and moot.

    The first recorded mention of this trend
was in the Briny Desert, at the end
of one terrific war we had to fight
against some human beings, for our right
to ransack their oasis for the Word.
That race of men had mimed some kind of bird.
No angels, these. Along their arms they grew
a flange of pinions, and with these they flew.[*]
Their feet were modified to grasping claws

---

[*]   *An angel's wing is much more deftly made:*
    a hypertrophic, feathered shoulder blade
    which makes him, technically a "hexopod"
    created by a special act of God.

4 ♦ The Apes of Eden: The Age of Thinkers

much like a hawk's. Instead of human jaws
they'd bone-hard lips, everted into beaks
with which their noses fused. These human freaks
built dwellings, like their congeners, but quite
distinctive: towers of enormous height.
They mainly occupied the upper floors,
and entered through the windows, not the doors.
In fact, though ground-floor entrances were found,
the only birds who entered at the ground
instead of windows many stories high
were those too young, or old, or sick, to fly.

    Not unexpectedly, they turned us down
when we requested leave to search their town,
and left us no alternative to war—
as nearly all their kind had done before.
We mounted yet another fell attack,
out-fought the harpies' flock, and drove them back
until they had to seek the safety of
the easily-defended spires above.
We found material for rams, and staved
the portals in, then resolutely braved
the boiling oil the harpies tried to pour
upon us as we climbed from "floor to floor"
—a term I use advisedly. Inside
each tower where the harpies tried to hide
we found one single undivided room
without a ceiling, which was seen to loom
at stellar altitude. Across this shaft
were two-by-fours, on which they perched and laughed -.
There were no "floors," just joists on which they hopped,
bespattered with the mess the birds had dropped.
The real floor was also heaped with moist,
fresh droppings, mostly underneath each joist.

    They laughed too soon. Since prehistoric time,
we apes have naturally known how to climb.
We scaled the crisscrossed two-by-fours with ease,

as if performing on the high trapeze,
while dodging missiles dropped from overhead
by desperate defenders as they fled.
We fought them to their topmost perches. There
they dived through windows, taking to the air.
They fled in all directions. Weeks went by
while we pursued, as far as they could fly.
When they by sheer exhaustion had been downed,
the braves of Eden slew them on the ground.

    When all of them were dead, we stopped a while,
and occupied their town, to live in style—
but not inside the messy, floorless towers
built for their convenience, not for ours.
Their stables, granaries and cowsheds were
—for comfort—quite a bit superior.

    As usual, we heard our Chief describe
the honor, might and glory of the Tribe,
while gathered braves' enthusiastic screech
provided punctuation for his speech.

    One ape, there was, inclined to disagree.
"Was genocide essential?" argued he.
"What tangible advantage have we gained
by making sure that not a soul remained?
These battles that we've almost always won
have paid off insults; but what have they done
toward realizing nobler tribal dreams?
Why must all skeptics die? To me it seems
there must be better ways to prove the truth
of our convictions to the world's uncouth.
Our victories keep heaping on my head
the tacit maledictions of the dead."

    This school of thought subsided rapidly
when we had hanged its founder to a tree.

    The Briny Desert was so aptly named!

6 ♦ The Apes of Eden: The Age of Thinkers

The only areas that could be tamed
by apes or human beings were a few
oases. Elsewhere nothing ever grew.
Between the scattered green spots on the plain
the only water fit to drink was rain
which almost never fell. We'd sometimes think
we'd found a lake or pond, and try to drink,
and learn that we could guzzle till we burst
without the least diminishing our thirst.

    The Tribe marched on. No stop was very long.
Discordant voices in our ranks grew strong;
and harsh suppression was no longer used
because the Chief himself became confused.
He knew dissent was wrong, but couldn't quite
decide which views were wrong and which were right.
If he endorsed one view, on private whim,
then all the Tribe might disagree with him;
and that, the Chief predicted, might be bad.
He wasn't quite the dumbest Chief we've had.

    Our days were spent in travel; but our nights
were spent in arguments, which led to fights.
We covered lots of philosophic ground
as well as salt flats. All our most profound
disquietude and speculation grew
from cosmic flaws that were so plain to view.
In such a universe as this one, could
there be a God omnipotent and good?
The blunders of creation seemed to be
too gross to be ascribed to Deity.

    Some tribesmen thought they could, and that this land
was good in ways too deep to understand.
Apparent flaws, which mortals counted odd,
revealed occult, unfathomed ways of God
Whose intellect performed at such a height
no ape could know what He considered right.

The very worst of sandstorms may be found
ideal for moving tons of sand around
to redistribute over other lands
for Purposes no mortal understands.
A rattlesnake—our racial enemy—
might benefit this sparse ecology
on desert lands, by thinning out some breed
of rodents who on vegetation feed
and—but for snakes—would overrun the land
and, by sheer numbers, strip it down to sand.
The fact these lands existed left no doubt
that their Creator relished dust and drought
for reasons which we hardly understood
but which, we could be sure, were Right and Good.

 This answer seemed to reaffirm God's powers,
but failed to prove He was a Friend of ours.

 So other sages, apes of high repute,
proposed this answer to the Great Dispute
which didn't satisfy the Tribe for long:
At first creation, nothing much was wrong;
till human tribes, and other misfit life,
had introduced an element of strife,
remolding Nature to their perverse tastes
(which seemed to run to arid, barren wastes),
or uglifying Nature with such tricks
as cutting mountains up in cubic bricks
to build their dwellings, as we'd seen them do.

 But there were grave objections to this view:
It might account for this or that detail,
but, generally applied, was quick to fail.
If drought was humans' handiwork, why, then,
was this "remodeled" land devoid of men?
The stony ruins were the humans' fault;
but could—or would—they turn the lakes to salt?

 Another theory, with a sounder base

in observation, was: the only place
that God Himself had made was Eden's land.
That might explain why immigrants were banned:
He wouldn't want His private hunting ground
despoiled by apes and beasts from all around.
The theory was that Lucifer had made
the world. To him, not God, the fault was laid.
This theory saved our faith in God's intent,
but made Him seem not-quite-omnipotent.

    A further difficulty with it was
the Tribe had left our ancient home because
we'd hoped to find the Deity somewhere.
We would, of course, have stayed, had God been there.
It wasn't very plausible to say
that God, disliking Eden, went away
to live in deserts Lucifer designed,
where mere subsistence was a chore to find.

    So tribal orthodoxy fell apart.
To build a new one, where was one to start?
Our only bond of gnostic unity
was that no two dissenters could agree,
and thus presented no "subversive cause"
that might have challenged Eden's tribal laws.
Our classic views remained at any rate
as starting points from which to deviate.
We had to tolerate dissent, because
we weren't quite sure what orthodoxy was.
We'd thought we knew; but now that questions were
debated openly, we weren't so sure.
Our theories needed data not supplied.
If we could find some facts, we could decide.
Our need for solid facts was growing strong.
We'd have to find some clues, before too long,
or Eden's long-enduring Tribe would be
beset with Crises of Identity.

THE PHILOSOPHICAL ENTERPRISE

As if the salt flat wasn't harsh enough,
the land we now approached was really rough.
We'd find no more oases; that we knew.
Beyond this last one, all that lay in view
was blistered desert, glowing hotly red—
all right for frying eggs, no place to tread.
A few intrepid scouts continued; then,
with toasted feet, came hopping back again.
As much as we'd have liked to forge ahead,
this natural barrier had stopped us dead.

    Until that time our custom was to steer
directly west, unless compelled to veer;
but what, exactly, is "Compulsion"? If
one comes upon a chasm, lake or cliff,
and no convenient way across is found,
one either has to stop, or go around.
One has to veer. But indications are
we sometimes let ourselves be swayed too far
too easily. Convenience, more than need,
determined which direction we'd proceed.
The humans also traveled on the plain
(for reasons crass, commercial and mundane),
so if we followed cart tracks here and there
across the sands, at least we got somewhere.
Although we'd find no dazzling truths to learn,
at least there'd be a town to sack and burn.
And, later on, when we resumed the Quest,

we chose a trail that led us almost west.

    A seeker after Truth should not avail
himself of every pre-established trail;
yet he who strikes out boldly on his own
may find himself forsaken and alone.
We tried that also, many times—at first—
and nearly died of hunger, heat and thirst.
In deserts there were no more clues to find
than in the settlements of humankind;
and trackless routes due westward often took
us into dull and dreary spots to look.
So who am I to say, in retrospect,
we never should have wandered, as we trekked?
Our forebears took whatever trail impressed
them as the quickest way to end the Quest.
The situation, now, was not the same.
The only trail led back the way we came.
Ahead lay desert, lifeless, stark and vast,
a prospect leaving even us aghast.
We clearly saw the fatal aftermath
of sticking to the Straight and Narrow Path;
yet actually admitting our mistake
and turning back, was more than we could take.
In tribal council, most of us agreed
we dared not forge ahead, nor yet recede.
That really left us no alternative
except to stop, and find some way to live
until some tribal genius had evolved
some means by which the problem could be solved.

    This was by far the longest of our stops.
We even tried our hand at planting crops.
We found a long-abandoned human town
and had, before we knew it, settled down,
postponing—week by week and year by year—
resuming our itinerate career.

Our Quest, it seemed, might be deferred a while.
Meanwhile, our Thirst for Knowledge to beguile,
we started sifting theologic facts
from long-accumulated scribal tracts.
It started with a sage of some renown,
who said, "We shouldn't let this get us down.
We've gathered information since the year
we left our tribal home, to end up here.
There must be something, in some tribal text,
that tells us how to go about it next.
It still might be a problem we can whip—
let's try some hermeneutic scholarship!"

With desert all around us, bleak and wide,
we'd little contact with the world outside—
a situation which inclined us more
to quiet scholarship than holy war.
For centuries, the best the Tribe could do
was inventory everything we knew
from records scribes had treasured since the age
when we were led from Eden by our Sage.
Our documents and sources, sad to say,
were largely myths from that forgotten day,
transcribed as told by gaffers of the Tribe,
somewhat revised by each successive scribe—
free-wheeling sagas of the Good Old Days
which different gaffers told in different ways,
and scribes embellished, either on their own,
or else from sources known to them alone.

Our tribal books are bulkier today
than once they were; but even then, they say,
the records we had kept of past events
made grist for dialectic eloquence.
The hints we'd heard, throughout the Hero Age,
were re-examined, word by line by page.
There wasn't much in tribal history
that helped us solve the Cosmic Mystery.

12 ♦ The Apes of Eden: The Age of Thinkers

Specific data that our scholars found
was often based on insubstantial ground.
The documents were scraps of stone and shell
which scribes had treasured long—but not as well
as one might wish. They'd been through many plights:
employed as missiles in the heat of fights,
regathered later—if they could be found—
stuffed back in sacks and ported all around.
A sack of rocks can come in handy. There's
a host of uses. Ours were used as chairs,
or heavy-duty blackjacks in a brawl.
The wonder is that they survived at all.
Those lost in war, catastrophe and storm
were later on recalled, in garbled form.
Odd bits of poetry turned up among
those strings of shells that broke, and were restrung;
and unexpected endings got attached
to songs and sagas that they hardly matched.
In time, of course, the archives came to be
a potpourri of myth and history—
a quarter ton of ill-assorted trash,
with one part truth to ten parts balderdash.

   Despite the nature of our documents
our efforts weren't without accomplishments.
We pieced together mutilated sherds
interpolating crucial missing words,
and thus ingeniously restored the lore
misplaced by scribes and chroniclers of yore.
Then theologians undertook to sleuth
these reconstructed records for the Truth.
By arts not known to every common clod,
they learned which scraps were valid words of God,
and which were altered, and to what extent,
and what the baffling contradictions meant.
Construing every passage twenty ways,
we left each other in a gnostic daze.

Manipulating jigsaw-puzzle texts
gave rise to multiplicity of sects.
We'd prove, by quoting some authority
in old, authentic codices (which we
devised by rearranging broken sherds)
mystiques for which we lacked expressive words,
inventing—then abusing—terms abstruse
which experts coined, expressly for this use.
By methods which to them alone were couth,
they'd wrestle out some grudging, makeshift Truth,
to use as premises for sound conclusions
free of errors, bias or delusions.

   Ages passed before we realized
what manuals of madness we'd devised.
Quite early in this period we faced
such questions as: On what is Knowledge based?
Can such a thing as Certitude exist?
In what does valid Evidence consist?
Can one be certain that the formal laws
of Logic don't embody subtle flaws?
What errors might some Higher Test detect
if Logic's rules are slyly incorrect?

   Those apes who'd spent their whole careers in search
of sound apologetics for the Church
were sometimes irked by questions such as these
and prone to brush them off as heresies;
but socially-responsive sages tried
to show that scholarship was justified.
They said although the Archives were in sad
condition, they were still the best we had.
By junking them completely, we'd forsake
our tribal Quest—a choice few apes would make. ·
And Logic, though depending heavily
upon the thinker's objectivity,
was still the way the pithecanic mind
was built to operate—as one would find

14 ♦ The Apes of Eden: The Age of Thinkers

trying to derive conclusions sure
through modes of thinking more or less impure.
At last our thinkers' purely-scholarly
research began to lose its novelty.
The climate of the times was growing ripe
for theologians of less formal type
who didn't think conclusions must perforce
depend upon a documented source.
The Naturalistic School of thought averred
that scribal lucubrations were absurd.

    "The proofs that God exists," they said, "abound,
if one will only take a look around;
for all about us, earth and sky and air
attest that Someone must have put them there."

    No logical objection could be found
to reasoning so manifestly sound,
until the Naturalistic School became
a self-refuting theologic game.
They couldn't rest content with what they'd proved,
but piled up theories many times removed
from observations tangible and clear
to which they still pretended to adhere.

    For instance, it was "obvious," they said,
the God must have at least one extra head,
so while Head One could get its sleep at night,
Head Two could guide the stars' nocturnal flight.
Another school could prove the heads were three.
Thus rose the Doctrine of the Trinity.
Some thought the tricephalic concept odd,
and settled for a polymorphous God—
one Aspect stayed in Heaven, one on Earth,
and one just sort of flitted back and forth;
and took no major action on his own,
his office being one of liaison.
Some theologues thought God was "One in Three,"

while some held out for "Threefold Unity."
Hard words arose between divergent schools,
who liked to call each other "threefold fools."

MS = MORE OF SAME

The haze began to lift when thinkers found
one doesn't really have to "look around."
Without supporting clues, or mental strain,
the "Light of Reason" brightened mortal brain.
They proved to us that Cosmic Deity,
by just the Nature of the Case, must be.

    Since God's a Perfect Being, every way,
it were a sheer absurdity to say
that anything He'd ever be or do
was less than Absolutely Perfect, too.
By definition, therefore, Deity
was That than Which no better thing could be;
it therefore follows (so that group believed)
God's nonexistence cannot be conceived.

    In simpler words, God must exist because
if He did not, His nonexistence was
the grossest imperfection, you'll agree,
and, ipso facto, contradictory.
Self-refutation's just as blatant, there,
as speaking of a round, or oval, square.

    A lot of mental energy was spent
to find a telling counterargument.
Although the reasoning was sound enough
for superficial readers, there were tough
objections by its critics. These arise
from wondering what "perfectness" implies.
If anything that's Perfect must exist
then where were all the Perfect things we missed:

the crops of Perfect vegetables and fruits;
the Perfect Sage, who never lost disputes?
In fact, some apes who partially encroach
on Perfectness are subject to reproach:
a globe—geometry's most Perfect shape—
is not considered graceful for an ape.

    Discussing Godly Attributes could bring
the theme around to almost anything.
E.g., was there a Perfect Rattlesnake
who must be lurking in the nearest brake?
(Ubiquity's an attribute, no doubt,
a Perfect Creature cannot do without.
Since he's imperfect if he "isn't there,"
it follows that he must be everywhere.)
Suppose there was. Would his Perfection be
what snakes thought perfect, or a sort that we
preferred in vermin we considered bad?
If so, he'd perish—or already had!
The obvious conclusion this implied
was that, since it was Perfect, it had died.
To blunder on, we must conclude at last
it can't be Perfect with a shady past,
which means—the pure logician will insist—
what's "perfect" is what never did exist.

    This reasoning was not designed to show
there was no God; it was a verbal blow
by one great sage against another one,
who soon replied that all the first had done
was show his own obtuseness to the world.
The counter-counterargument he hurled
was that his critics had completely missed
the point, to say he'd said all things exist
in Perfect Forms. No rattlesnake is good
for anything; that should be understood.
And if it isn't good, it must be bad;
and there goes every ground your thesis had.

18 ♦ The Apes of Eden: The Age of Thinkers

If snakes had any perfect attribute,
then what to call them is the main dispute.
This inconsistent quality would make
it something else; it wouldn't be a snake.
No theorist had ever yet attacked
the view that God existed. That was fact.
But even proving that the truth was true
gave thinkers quite a lot of work to do.
In order to construct a valid case,
one stacks deductions on a solid base
of fact, on which the sage begins his task.
But there are reams of questions he must ask
before he gets his thesis off the ground;
and, for them all, the answers must be found.
If all objections aren't disposed of first,
then rival sages quickly do their worst.
The greater a philosopher's renown,
the harder others worked to pull him down.
They even found some unexpected flaws
in what we call the Proof from Natural Laws.
It goes like this: One never does observe
the universe from certain laws to swerve .
Live grass is always green. All apes are brown.
A fall, from any height, is always down.
The night is always dark; all days are light.
No object's visible, that's out of sight.
The winter's always cool; the summer's warm.
The wind has mass, but no distinctive form,
and always moves. A wind just sitting there
immobile must revert to common air.
Since there are laws of nature, there must be
some Ruler to enact them by decree.
You'll recognize the school of thought our Sage
in Eden founded, in that golden age
before the Exodus. It's stood the test
of centuries. Some say it's still the best.

Of course we'd modified it quite a bit
as new sophistication honed our wit.
Our Sage in Eden thought the world was "good,"
with "laws of nature" working as they should—
a rash assumption, later on debunked
by hard experience, and finally junked.
But though the universe was full of flaws
no ape could doubt that it was run by laws;
the only difference was, the laws we've made
we break, while Nature can't be disobeyed.
These ratiocinations weren't enough
when clever sophists got to do their stuff.
The so-called "laws" of Nature, they opined
existed mainly in the thinker's mind.
When one equates a "Natural Law" with one
our Chief makes up, it's nothing but a pun.
Its wording doesn't necessarily
reflect a basis in Reality.
Two ones would equal just exactly two
if God had never told them what to do.
No "natural law" is thus exemplified;
it's just a designation we've applied
to integers whose cardinality
is more than unity and less than three.

    To say that "down" is "whither objects fall"
is definition—not a law at all.
So even laws of physics are defined
by process of the pithecanic mind.
They're mere descriptions of the tendencies
that any ape observing nature sees.
They're paths of least resistance. That you've got
regardless whether God exists or not.

    We have a tendency to generalize,
and say that stars are "always" in the skies,
while lights like lightning bugs and campfire flames
are not. Again we're just applying names.

20 ♦ The Apes of Eden: The Age of Thinkers

The "Law" consists of definitions of
those lights we see on Earth, and those above.
Which light may not, or may, be labeled "star"
depends on nothing more than where they are.
If Natural Order's ever disarranged
our terminology is promptly changed,
imposing on the world a "lawfulness"
it doesn't necessarily possess.
A "star" on Earth would violate no Law;
we'd simply change the name of what we saw.

    The order of the seasons, which you say
is evidence of Providence's sway,
is just the set of labels we impose
on cyclical phenomena like those.
If fall preceded summer, we would call
it "spring," so it would not be fall at all.

    You say the stars would wander from their course
unless restrained by supernatural force.
Although we may not know the reason why
they fly from east to west across the sky,
it's just as plausible to say they whiz
along the route where least resistance is.
If next you say the way they are aligned
in Constellations is by God designed,
why couldn't some philosopher advance
the theory that they're strewn around by chance?
What sort of Natural Law can you devise
explaining their arrangement in the skies?

    Besides, as most observant apes recall,
the stars are sometimes even known to fall.
This further undermines your argument,
implying God is not omnipotent,
or doesn't care. Nor can you rationalize
and say He didn't want them in the skies
and let them fall; for that's a premise drawn

from your conclusion—not itself foregone.
You cannot win a logical debate
with arguments which frankly circulate!

    When critics chose to argue tooth and claw
it never took them long to find a flaw
in any theory any sage advanced;
so Certitude was never much enhanced.

    I'm sure that's where the basic problem lies,
which killed the Philosophic Enterprise.
Our search for Truth and Understanding led
to academic free-for-alls instead.
Through all the years our tribal thinkers wove
their wondrous webs of thought, they also strove
to bring each other's theories to disgrace,
and make the worse appear the better case.

PHD = PILED HIGH AND DEEP

Contriving ever more ingenious ways
to cure the theological malaise,
we found that proof for God's existence lurked
within our psyches.
                              This is how it worked:
For all those things of which an ape is fond
some complements in Nature correspond.
For instance, we would never feel the mood
to eat, if there were no such thing as food.
We wouldn't comprehend the sense of thirst
if God had not created water first.
On chilly desert nights, an ape's desire
for warmth implies there's such a thing as fire.
Existence of the Procreative Urge
implies that unlike sexes can converge.
New things to learn and know must surely be
to complement our curiosity;
and all the countless leagues our Tribe had trod
in search of Him, implies that there's a God.
The fact that we've been willing to pursue
our tribal dream, implies it must be true.
(This proof collapsed, when someone made a list
of things he yearned for, which did not exist.)

    Another sage of keen and subtle wit
maintained the concept of an Infinite
and Perfect Being (as distinguished from
mere definitions of Him) could become

a sounder proof than offered heretofore.
Since neither data from the senses, nor
the structure of the finite mortal mind
would be a very likely place to find
examples of Perfection Absolute,
one must look elsewhere for this Concept's root.

    Since no effect lacks cause, we realize
our concept of The Perfect must arise
from somewhere. Possibilities are three:
(A) pithecan imagination; (B)
the world outside our minds; and (C) the thing
itself. But since a finite cause can bring
effects no more than finite, who can doubt
that causes (A) and (B) are weeded out?
An ape—a very finite, mortal clod—
could ex nihilo imagine God;
nor could this transcendental concept's cause
be somewhere in a cosmos rife with flaws.
So, since the Cause must equal its effect,
we know the Concept comes from God, direct.

    His carping critics set to work, to show
he'd proven nothing that we didn't know.
Our thinker tells us where the Concept's from,
but doesn't say by what strange route it's come.
God won't communicate in any sense;
and won't provide objective evidence.
Our author presupposes God's intent
to give our race a theologic bent
by planting in our minds a sort of lure
to seek for That of Which we're never sure.
But if this were the case, it might be nice
to make the Concept lucid and precise.

    His implication that the Infinite
can never be conceived by mortal wit
is somewhat imprecise. We do surmise

a lot of things we cannot visualize.
How many cubs, who've never seen a snark,
imagine they can hear one in the dark?
We can't imagine what it's like in Hell;
and yet it's easy to pronounce and spell.
We cannot visualize the universe,
although the word is very clear and terse,
supplying "concepts" which can be discussed,
although we've no description we can trust.
The symbol that we often use to "state"
the Infinite, is just a "lazy eight,"
which obviously isn't infinite—
a single penstroke will encircle it.
And yet a symbol "written in the mind"
is not by finite brain and skull confined?

    It doesn't follow, then, from logic's laws
that all effects are equal to their cause.
While some effects are greater, some are less;
the cause itself is often just a guess.
Though God exists, the fact's not clear from these
mere symbols, stacked to build hypotheses.

    The problem of Theodicy remained.

    "This universe is best," one sage maintained.
"Disasters, reptiles, drought and sickness can
be God's creations, vital to His Plan.
An Infinite and Perfect Being must
be powerful—but also Kind and Just.
We've wracked out brains for explanations for
creation's flaws, which living things deplore.
The answer's clear, if we apply our wits—
a matter of contrasting opposites!
No secret "higher Purpose" need be found
for Evil things which in this world abound.
In any universe God might create
there's automatically an average state

of "neutral" value. Most of what we see
must deviate from this, to some degree.
We view as "good" all things with Value more
than neutral things, whose value we ignore.
Those objects, states and creatures which are worse
than "normal" for a certain universe
are necessarily as Evils viewed—
the only realistic attitude.

   God did create a Better Sphere above
where life's a bed of roses, bliss and love;
but if we lived there, might we not be seen
as troublemakers, ugly, dumb and mean?
Down here, we apes are fairly virtuous,
since every other breed is worse than us;
and yet we have our imperfections, too,
which might stand out, from higher points of view.
If Evil were eradicated, we
—not snakes—would be the Moral Perigee!
Who wants to live with angels, and be viewed
as paragons of Moral Turpitude?

   In Heaven there's no hardship, toil or pain;
but states that we think "neutral" do remain
when nothing's happening Might angels see
such "lulls in bliss" as boring misery?
Obversely, hellfiends hold the fond belief
that life on Earth would be a big relief.
In other words, we meaninglessly prate
that God a "better" cosmos should create,
when any cosmos He created would
contain some Bad, some Average, and some Good.
The sole alternative to this would be
a wholly-neutral, dull monotony;
for even residents of Heaven's Sphere
still have the wrath of Deity to fear.
Nor, on the other hand, would things seem worse
to natives of an "evil" universe;

where, just as here on Earth, some average state
all Good and Evil would discriminate.
So let's accept the fact that Good and Bad
in balance are the best that can be had;
for how could Up exist, if Down did not?
Could anything be Cold, if nothing's Hot?
Were there no Evil, there could be no Good;
and so the world is running as it should.
(As if one said, Until the flood gets high
the land beneath it can't be truly dry.)

    Those apes were sharp, I've come to realize;
and here's a proof that takes the Nobel Prize.
It draws its methodology from the
symbology of simple algebra.
This scholar starts his somewhat-lengthy tract
by segregating Undisputed Fact
from highly-questionable inference
derived inductively from Evidence.
Our logical constructions seem quite grand,
but metaphysically are built on sand
for want of postulates. Theology
is therefore whirled away in sophistry.
The problem in substantiating God
[he writes] is lack of any canon rod
by which Divinity can be defined
in terms within the grasp of finite mind.
We know He's not confined to any place.
His Being fills the vasty depths of space.
There isn't any place He doesn't go,
nor any knowledge that He doesn't know.
Whatever God might wish to do, He could.
He's infinitely potent, wise and good.
In short, He's "infinite"; and that's a word
we cannot grasp, however often heard.
Although its meaning may be well defined,
the concept is beyond a finite mind;

and this explains [our author next insists]
why no one yet has proven God exists.

    Theology's persistent nemesis
is lack of fundamental premises.
If X is Y, and every Y is Z,
then X an element of Z must be.
That's all intuitively clear. The hitch
is knowing which of these is fact, and which
mere speculation. Our theology
is grounded in epistemology
and metaphysics; and, if these aren't sound,
then where can valid premises be found?
We have to act as if there were no doubt
that God is something one can think about
concretely; but in this we're like the ant
who "grasps" a mountain. Naturally he can't
except in trivial detail. He'll touch
one minor aspect, never learning much.
Yet this is what our theologues have done
in treating Godly aspects, one by one,
in which misplaced expenditure of wit
they "grasp" one aspect of the Infinite,
neglecting utterly to take account
of all the others, boundless in amount.
So every "proof" mere verbal schemes begat
has either vaporized or fallen flat.
Some other ant has "grasped" a different place
and seen another aspect of the case.
We need some means whereby a finite dunce
can comprehend the Boundless, all at once.

    And here this writer's central theme is broached.
The way the subject ought to be approached
is through a methodology which spans
the endless gap from God to pithecans.
And that is Mathematics—known to be
the Basic Substrate of Reality.

All matter, space and time, effect and cause
are governed by its flawless, changeless laws.
Its verities, in symbols clear and terse,
are independent of the universe,
controlling Nature and the Mind of God
as well as those who tread this earthly sod.
The scholar trusting what he hears and sees
makes Errors, which result in fallacies.
Consulting Scripture has its pitfalls, too:
we can't be absolutely sure it's true;
besides the fact that, even if we were,
we can't be sure of its interpreter.
But Mathematics, formal and exact,
consists of absolute, undoubted Fact.
This closest thing to Certitude we've got
would still exist if all the world did not.
Its truths, perceived directly by the mind,
are a priori certainties. To find
a trigon's angles to be four or two
is one thing even God could never do.
In fact, the more omniscient and wise,
the more a mind on Basic Truth relies;
one therefore hears philosophers refer
to "God, the Ultimate Geometer."
Whatever else Reality may be
no two-plus-two will ever equal three;
and anyone who finds the wrong amount
proves only that he never learned to count.
Desist, therefore, from methods vague and crude!
Proceed to algebraic certitude!

    The primal Nothingness from which the world
took form and mass, and into Being swirled
is represented, as you might expect,
by Zero—arithmetically correct.
By contrast, Infinite Divinity
is represented by ∞.

The set of all existent objects seems
to lie between these opposite extremes,
so physical reality is then
depicted algebraically as N.
A lemma: We must prove infinity
is generated arithmetically.
(This doesn't mean, of course, that God derives
from finite being; but our author strives
to show by methods clear to finite wit
that zero into N is infinite.)

    By definition, any ratio R
is numerator N (above the bar)
divided by another quantity
(below the bar), denominator D.
N over D, whatever size they are
will yield a ratio, which we write as R.
By arithmetic law, the product when
we multiply this D times R, is N.
Example: N is six and D is three.
There's nothing else but two that R can be;
so two times three is six. The rule's the same
for any choice of constants you can name.
We see that larger Ns, or smaller Ds,
will make our R however large we please.
As D becomes a microscopic mote,
the graph of R describes an asymptote.
As D approaches zero, R is found
abruptly to expand beyond all bound.
If N is positive, the vanished trace
of D makes R explode in someone's face.
Since 0 into N is boundless, then
∞ times zero equals N.

    N, generated by ∞
thus proves that Infinite Divinity
created all the cosmos: "Something" wrought
from "Nothing" by the power of His thought.

Devise whatever arguments you please,
your critics ferret out the fallacies.
We might have had a proof that God exists
except for carping by semanticists,
who all, for motives of their own, preferred
to split a hair about a single word.
The "ratio R," another sage opined,
was not "unbounded;" it was "undefined."

    The next dead end on which some time was spent
was called the "Cosmologic Argument."
The premise—garnered from experience—
was that a chain of physical events
connects all happenstance, without a pause,
so everything that happens has a cause.
This cause in turn was caused, and so, immersed
in fogs antique, was That Which Happened First.
A pod grows seeds, which grow another pod,
around and 'round—but What Came First was God.
This left some pious souls dissatisfied,
and led some rival sages to decide
that what these thinkers called the Deity
was metaphysical monstrosity.
Its shape and nature lurked in ancient mist.
All we could know was that "It" must exist.
That things began somewhere is plain to see;
but can we call that Somewhere "Deity"?

    At least, they claimed, it proves the Logos is,
and all creation, therefore, must be His.
The counter-quibble, then, was that the past
need have no First, as future has no Last.
The dreadful premise this must rest upon
is that the stream of time goes on and on,
and on ... and on ... and on, without a break;
but that's where sanity begins to quake!

    Conversely, let's assume that time will end;

there'll be some point past which it can't extend.
Again imagination drops us flat;
we can't help asking, "What comes after that?"
Suppose time did begin. One question more:
Since time itself could not exist before
the primal Unmoved Mover played His part
how, then, could even God know when to start?
The thinkers had to let these questions go;
so, if you find the answers,
let me know.

AN ESSAY ON MORALS

You should have heard our thinkers go the rounds
on Ethics and its theologic grounds,
in scholarly, and bitter, verbal strife
about what constitutes the Moral Life.
The three most urgent questions on our list
were, first and foremost, Does a God exist?
and second, Can we Free Volition find
in mechanistic functions of the mind?
but all the toughest arguments we had
concerned What constituted Good and Bad.

    One area where no two apes agree
is that of Ethics, or Morality.
The question, What ought one to do? was found
to be an issue we could kick around
as long as tempers held, and never make
the slightest headway, nor a deadlock break .
We wracked our brains for centuries on end
to figure out: On what does Good depend—
on Pleasure, Duty, Harmony or Love,
the Will of God, or none of the above?
Is Good a mere contingent quality
which apes can only sense subjectively;
or does a thing itself have what one could
call an "inherent" or "objective" Good?
An object's "value" isn't evident
objectively to any great extent
unless it shines or glitters, and displays
its trinket-value in objective ways;
yet one persistent habit in the Tribe

is "value" to dead objects to ascribe.

    Philosophy had been, till then, concerned
with what (if anything) the Tribe had learned
about the Nature of Reality
with special focus on theology.
Regrettably, however hard we tried
to stick to this, the subject ramified.
The reason for the sidetrack was that creeds
then current, came to stress the worth of deeds
as well as True Belief, to save one's soul.
Defining "worth" became the thinkers' goal
because our preachers always disagreed
about which moral tenets one should heed.
They had to clash, in order to protect
the unique purity of every sect;
so sages had to figure out the Good
and True and Beautiful, or no one could.
Besides, our writers on philosophy
found definitions a necessity,
and therefore had the expertise one needs
not found among adherents of the creeds.
Such terms as "right" and "good," when loosely used
made Reasoning grow tangled and confused.
No accusation made a scholar squirm
like that of having "not defined a term"
in his exhaustive monograph, involved
with every question hitherto unsolved,
so that, instead of winning just applause,
his work was merely laughed at for its flaws.

    Though Good and Bad are told apart with ease,
one gets entangled in priorities
in any case of which it's fair to say
it's neither Black nor White, but murky gray.
Moreover, to predict the end result
of good and evil deeds, is difficult;
and sometimes Righteous Acts are later found

with Evil Consequences to abound.
The problem is that "benefit" derives
from leading somewhat less-than-moral lives.
The fact that chiselers oftentimes succeed
in life, while honest apes end up in need
has been a source of disillusionment
since ancient times, for apes of good intent.
Not only that, but Adverse Fortune could
pass over scoundrels and assail the good—
another case of seeming Cosmic Flaws
that made us wonder whether Nature's Laws
(the ones alleged to prove that God exists)
were fabrications by our theorists.
The question was inevitably raised
of whether "morals" had been misappraised
so that the "good" and "bad" we apes believed
we saw in objects, we'd ourselves conceived;
and whether certain of the rules we had
for differentiating Good from Bad
were either false, or poorly understood.

So thinkers reexamined what was "good"
and found the problem thorny. Some opined
that "good" could scarcely even be defined,
and that they'd all be very much surprised
it anyone could get it analyzed.

The terms are various. Key words are "good"
and "value." Common verbs are "ought" and "should"
—though these are quickly redefined to give
their definitions through some adjective:
We "ought" to do what's "good" or "right" to do,
and "should" as tantamount to "ought" construe.
Both verbs to "obligation" are resolved,
so Value Judgments always get involved
before the circumspect philosopher
to anything objective can refer.
The omnipresent danger is, in these,

that they'll reduce to Circularities.
Though Up and Down we readily define
by reference to a mason's weighted line,
our Good and Evil commonly relate
to Should and Shouldn't—so they circulate,
since "should" and "ought" must be in turn defined
with "values"—products of the thinker's mind.
The frequency with which this has occurred
in treatises on Ethics, is absurd.

    These "value words," although it may seem odd,
confuse the Thinking Ape, but not the clod.
A moron knows by Instinct what they mean;
but they're in subtle applications seen,
where terminology must be precise
and brainless Intuition won't suffice.
The "value" of a pound of beans or tea
is not the "value" of Morality.
The "value" of a poem isn't quite
the same as that of some religious rite.
All these are "good," but good in ways where we
cannot define the similarity.
The first in coins or trade-goods is defined;
the second use describes a turn of mind;
the third uplifts one's soul, esthetically;
the fourth helps apes commune with Deity
or puts some deep Religious Truth across
for which, with words alone, we're at a loss.
The axiologist must now confirm
that there's a general meaning for the term.

    So much for "Good" as generality;
our present topic is Morality.
Although simplistic Moral Codes abound,
in each some ambiguities are found,
allowing apes of Pharisaic mind
the faults of others, not themselves, to find.
Most answers to the question, What to do?

are merely slogans: "To thyself be true,"
or "Drown thy woes in revelry and song,"
or "Cherish what is Right, and shun what's Wrong"
or "Do as law and custom tell you to,"
or "Do as you'd have others do to you."
One cannot live by shibboleths like these
without a system of Priorities;
and any way the problem is attacked
this is exactly what the slogans lacked.

    Pursuing Right and Shunning Wrong is fine,
until your rights and wrongs conflict with mine;
and then confusion reigns. Our Moral Rights
are frequent grounds for arguments and fights
wherein each party is completely sure
his rationale is virtuous and pure.

    That's why a thinker I shall later cite
insists that mindless Force defines what's "right"
—for reasons even Killer Apes should see
holds little water, philosophically.
A conflict does more harm than good, if it
results in no one's real benefit.
Both "A" and "B" are righteous. Both mean well.
Mere lack of common rights and wrongs compel
their "Last Resort" to strife which neither chose,
and turned good neighbors into mortal foes.
"A" perished; "B" survived. Each had to fight
in brave defense of what he knew was Right—
both justified in their conflicting needs
according to their private moral creeds.
Suppose that "A" was right, and "B" was not.
The issue's settled, but what have we got?
Each fought for what he knew was Just and True,
but "A" lies dead, while "B" is black and blue
and gloats about his well-won Moral Wreath
while limping homeward, counting broken teeth.

This is a Moral Situation, and
a case we have to try to understand:
Has Evil really triumphed; or has "B"'s
mistake been punished with his injuries?
Is "A" rewarded—since we know he must
have taken solace, ere he bit the dust,
in knowing that, by cosmic standards, he,
and not his foe, deserved the victory?
Was "B" rewarded for his being wrong?
Does God assist the evil and the strong,
or will "B" suffer for his past mistakes
in future quarrels that he undertakes?

    Now let's suppose that "B" was in the right
by some objective canon. Can we quite
condone his carrying to such extremes
what he as moral Truth and Justice deems,
or did he, at some juncture in the brawl,
surpass his moral duty's righteous call
and let his Instincts—being what they are—
supplant Pure Ethics, as his Guiding Star?
If so, should tribal sanctions be applied,
since by his hand a fellow ape has died;
or does his being in the Right outweigh
his having done more harm than good, that day?
If not, then can his aches and fractures be
a fair reward for Rightful Victory
in quarrels which should never have occurred?

    Some common Standard would have been preferred,
not only from a Cosmic point of view
but for our tribal strength and welfare, too.
Our tribal code was written to prevent
such loss of life through "moral accident."

    The moral implication is, of course,
that Wrong can oftentimes prevail, by force;
and Deity, with Wisdom Infinite,

will seldom deign to get involved in it.
So combat, most philosophers agree,
while settling quarrels, holds no guarantee
that he whose fists and fortunes win the fight
is—in perspective—either wrong or right.

An Essay on Morals (Concluded)

Although our tribal code is full of flaws,
we benefit from arbitrary laws;
so here's another Guiding Light for you:
"Do just as law and custom tell you to!"

    Though stupid laws will do more good than none,
few apes agreed that all was said and done,
once laws were made. We felt that Nature owed
the Tribe a Universal Moral Code.
But what is "right" or "good" has much to do
with idiosyncratic points of view.
"One tribesman's meat's another's poison," and
"What's sauce for geese may not be sauce for gand
ers." Moral thinkers floundered all around,
but couldn't get their feet on solid ground.
A scribe sees "value" in a piece of stone
beyond the "innate good" of rock alone:
A slab of rock—a bulky nuisance to
the ploughboy—may be "valuable" to you
for being tablet-shaped, with the exact
dimensions you may need to write a tract.
A stone upon the path is "neutral"—though
it turns Malicious when you stub your toe.

    If Strength is not our standard, might Success
in Life extract us from this sophic mess?
The theory is that God rewards the good
by helping them obtain their livelihood;

which indicates, when all is said and done,
that God decrees: "Look out for Number One!"
The "Social Darwinism" this implies
sounds better to the rich than to the wise,
reminding us of several clear cut flaws
in "social orders" based on teeth and claws.
We toil and scheme, and each of us derives
the most we can from our respective lives.
Some apes are spendthrift, others try to save;
but all end up with nothing, in the grave.
When apes have everything on earth they need
yet keep on striving, this is known as "greed."
If other apes, who are content with less,
avoid the rat-race, that's called "shiftlessness."
Since Greed and Sloth are both immoral, may
we seek perfection in the Middle Way?
Few recommend that course; the Golden Mean
as lukewarm "wishy-washiness" is seen.
It's evident that any course we take
impresses others as a Big Mistake.

   "Good" sometimes fluctuates. Such "goods" as foods
depend on evanescent attitudes,
appearing "better" as one breaks a fast
than after stuffing down a rich repast.
Some "good" is not inherent, we conclude,
but stems from one's subjective attitude.
Does every "good" and "evil" therefore rise
from how it's viewed through someone's biased eyes,
like Left and Right, which, if regarded from
new viewpoints, their own opposites become?
This last was very quickly seen to be
a problem in epistemology:
Do flowers which "inherently" are blue
appear to someone else of different hue?—
a question leading someone to remark
that nothing's any color in the dark.

If nothing's good or bad inherently
unless some ape perceives its quality,
do falling rocks, or thunder, make no sound
if no one who can hear them is around?

    Yet this Subjectivistic Ethic seems
preposterous, if carried to extremes:
Sound sleep is obviously Good, although
until the sleeper wakes, he doesn't know
if he's enjoying it or not. Therefore
it's "unperceived," unless he starts to snore.
Might God become an "evil" to despise
if apes did not perceive Him otherwise?
This is absurd, but has to be agreed
if good and evil from ourselves proceed.
We're driven to conclude Inherent Good
exists, if it's correctly understood;
and variations in our attitude
prove only that our Value Sense is crude.
We strove by application of the mind
to make our apperceptions more refined;
but all our efforts, as it now appears,
were stymied for another thousand years.

    A dozen inconsistencies arise
from stating that The Good in pleasure lies—
the classic Hedonistic point of view.
It seems, intuitively, to be true
that Good brings pleasure and that Bad brings pain;
yet problematic instances remain.
Enjoyment comes in many different ways—
from food, possessions, health, and others' praise.
It comes and goes as slyly as an elf,
as indefinable as "good" itself.
An altruistic ape, for instance, may
take more delight in giving things away
than in obtaining them; so some believe
"It better is to give than to receive;"

while egocentric apes are merely bored
when told that "Virtue is its own reward."

    Another Snag arises when we find
that tribesmen with a certain turn of mind
enjoy the feeling of disliking things—
no other sentiment such pleasure brings.
No precious gem exists, by which they're awed;
it's either ostentatious, or it's flawed.
The fellow tribesmen whom they most despise
are those who have no faults to criticize.
Although no pleasure pleases them a bit,
they do take pleasure in disliking it.

    Our scribes and poets praise the heroes bold
who lived and fought and died in days of old;
and storytellers fervidly describe
how ancient heroes glorified the Tribe.
Their deeds must surely be accounted "good;"
and yet it's hard to see how "pleasure" could
be readily derived from martial strife
and other hardships of a hero's life.
This is explained, the hedonist will say,
as "pleasant" in an altruistic way;
they know that other apes, who benefit
from tribal glory, are enjoying it.
Besides, some Killer Apes take keen delight
from the exhilaration of a fight.
So "pleasure" must be slightly redefined
to make allowance for this turn of mind.

    But martyrs, known to human history
have died by torment voluntarily,
although no "pleasure" from such deaths could be
derived by them, nor by posterity.
The hedonist explains that martyrs take
some strange delight from burning at the stake.
But "stretching definitions till they fit"

is just an exercise in verbal wit;
for when we're asked what "pleasure" is, we could
define it as "reaction to The Good."
Another vicious circle is obtained;
and not a jot of understanding gained.

   One fine distinction must be understood:
there's instrumental and intrinsic Good.
No "pleasure" came from hoeing corn all day,
yet nothing else would keep the weeds at bay.
The weeds were not "innately" good or bad,
and had the selfsame "rights" our cornstalks had—
except that "noxious" weeds' unchallenged growth
would crowd the corn; there wasn't room for both.
And, since uncrowded cornstalks in one's field
produced what we would call a "better" yield
(which meant we'd more to eat), it's understood
that hoeing corn's an "instrumental" Good .
An "instrument" to what? The goal pursued
in farming's nothing more nor less than Food;
and food, like other useful forms of wealth,
enhances and prolongs one's life and health.
So hoeing corn, however onerous
it seems, is ultimately "good" for us.

   Now food a "good" and worthy purpose serves,
since life is "good," and that's what food preserves.
But food is also "instrumental" in
such ends as Gluttony—a mortal sin.
The same holds true in asking what we gain
from riches—for the wealthy and the vain.
Few apes would doubt that wealth consists of "goods"
—which are, of course, synonymous with "shoulds,"
as we explained some paragraphs ago.
The rich, however, do deserve to know
what sort of moral swamp they wander in,
for wealth is Vanity—another Sin.

An "instrumental snag" is, Charity
(kind gifts to those possessing less than we)
may just prolong some miserable life
beset with illness, poverty and strife,
for which the kindest thing we could have done
might be to hasten Sweet Oblivion.
Yet putting someone out of misery
conflicts with laws on which we all agree:
that killing fellow tribesmen isn't Right
except in self defense. This shows the plight
well-meaning apes confronted when they had
to make a choice—and every choice was Bad.
One clear (perhaps simplistic) rule to use
is: "Lesser over greater evil choose!"
A saint, confronting some Dilemma's horns,
the short horn chooses and the long one scorns.
The ape who makes the least immoral choice
may in Umblemished Virtue still rejoice.
For instance, if one has to tell a lie
to right some Wrong, this Precept would apply.
To kill is wrong, but if one's life's at stake,
one must a stern and just Decision make,
and virtuously do what must be done:
Defend thyself—Look out for Number One!

Again, it's wrong to steal; but when in need
we few concessions make to misers' greed.
Your need is dire; you know he has enough
and some to spare—he'll never miss the stuff.
But first be sure that Life's Inequities
will be corrected by your thieveries.
If he's not rich, or if your need's not real,
the Precept still applies: It's wrong to steal.
But "wealth" can be subjective. What to me
looks opulent, may seem like "poverty"
to other apes, who used to have much more
and now have less than they possessed before.

It's therefore hard to be completely sure
which victims of your theft are rich or poor.
The same applies to "poverty." Your Need
is self-appraised, and hard to tell from Greed—
especially by victims of your theft
who always think they worked for What Just Left.

   Another pitfall is, it's difficult
to know a well-meant action's End Result.
To pull a drowning tribesman from a well
is hardly wicked; but how can one tell
what later evil he may perpetrate
if "virtuously" rescued from his fate?
To save a scoundrel who's about to drown
might make you Malefactor of the Town.
To saunter off and leave him might have been
to spare the world from some outrageous sin.
We can't predict this, yet we must decide:
It might have hurt your Conscience, had he died.
The merit of your deed is up to Fate,
whose whims we rarely know, until too late.

   "Do unto others as you'd have them do
(in similar conditions) unto you!"
This makes good sense. The Golden Rule provides
the moral-minded ape with clear-cut guides,
and strikes the Ethics quandary at the root.

   In application, though, it's sometimes moot.
Too much of "what they'd have you do" depends
on other tribesmen's choice of worthy ends,
which may assume some unexpected shapes
within your mind, or those of other apes.
There are some apes we simply cannot trust
to choose amusements for themselves. We must
restrain their movements; and we take alarm
at what they're doing, lest they come to harm.
Small cubs are one example; also those

adults who can't contend with natural foes
and other hazards they'll encounter while
their bent for reckless rambles they beguile,
by reason of advanced senility
or mental irresponsibility.
Restraining them by force is not "to do
as you would have such people do to you;"
so, as regards incompetents and fools,
we make exceptions to this Best of Rules.
Your beneficiary's perverse taste
may mean your well-meant kindness goes to waste.
Suppose you're fond of some unique repast
which leaves your squeamish dinner guests aghast.
The Golden Rule again is seen to fail
if with third helpings you your friends regale,
which—lest you take offense—they must consume
despite a sense of gastronomic doom.

    If you on self-destruction were intent,
my helping hand, however kindly meant,
would be resented. What, then, should you do
if someone else refuses aid from you?
You know he's psychologically deranged
and that his mood, by morning, may have changed.
The Golden Rule, however, states that you
must do to him as you would have him do:
in this case, leave him be. Stand idly by
and watch your suicidal tribesman die.
You know by other apes you'll be condemned,
although your choice from Moral Law has stemmed.

    A lot of us would tend to falter here,
forget the Golden Rule, and interfere.

    "The Will of God is right; all else is wrong;
so do His Will with testimony strong!"

    This follows logically, as well it should,
from our assumption of "Objective Good"—

that in each act or object we may find
some "value" independent of the mind.
Since all existing things are God's designs,
their Value is whatever He defines.
Not only objects, but each act and thought
is Good or Evil as He may have wrought.
When Moral Laws are legislated by
the Deity, one doesn't wonder why;
one needn't ask Him why He feels that way—
one simply grins, and rushes to obey.

    This value system saves us mental strain,
because (although dilemmas still remain)
we never have to wonder what is Right.
The thinking's done, and put in black and white
by those who are more competent than we
to know what is ordained by Deity.
The pious ape need only sift through loads
of varied, and conflicting, Moral Codes
which rival sects propound; and then decide
by which of these—if any—to abide.

    His "testimony" tells him which is best;
and he, with no misgivings, junks the rest—
then finds he's universally condemned,
because his Standards from himself have stemmed,
as if he were an irreligious clod
who never heard about the Will of God,
and thinks the Spirit of the Law's confused
with its imperfect wording, and abused.
But, knowing when he's Right, he sets his jaw
and isn't swayed by less-than-Godly law,
until, adhering to his True Belief,
he runs afoul of edicts by our Chief.

    The problem of defining "Good" remains
among philosophy's persistent banes.
Despite the brief successes thinkers had
the problem was, itself, completely Bad.

THE GIFT OF PROPHESY

When scholars failed, another type arose:
the Messenger of God, the One Who Knows—
the Prophet who, disdaining argument,
serenely fills the role for which he's Sent.
Our prophets had no need to think things through,
for they the truths of Earth and Heaven knew
direct from God, and thus could not be caught
in captious vagaries of mortal thought.

    The tacit base of their philosophy
was that the Rational Mentality
was devilish, misleading and uncouth—
less help than hindrance in pursuit of Truth.
Instead of thinking, let us put our faith
in what the God-instructed prophet saith.

    Through erudition we could not be reached,
but now that gap was bridged, as prophets preached
their gospels up and down throughout the land
in terms the dumbest apes could understand:

    "Don't let yourselves by thinking be beguiled.
You won't be saved unless you're like a child!
Ignore all others; get your facts from me!
You'll know the Truth, and Truth will make you free!"

    Debunking the "pretensions of the wise"
gave know-the-truths the right to improvise
with logic rough and ready—mostly rough.
Their hearts were right, and that was good enough.
However mortal Reason might detract
from what they said, they had the Gospel Fact;

and woe betide the ape enmired in Doubt
too deeply for his Faith to pry him out.
Their instant truths, so easy to obtain,
made few demands upon the toiling brain.
The prophets brought the eager multitude
no lumpy Data, needing to be chewed,
but nicely sugared, predigested pulp
that one could swallow at a single gulp.
In fact, when lumps were found, our prophets taught
that these were catalyzed by too much Thought.
The Truth goes down more easily, we'd find,
if we'd accept it "with an open mind."
With just a little practice, we believed
whatever fantasies the proph's conceived.
They freed us from the chains of Evidence
and from the tyranny of Common Sense.

   What reasoning they did was quite direct
and worthy of a thinking ape's respect,
if not complete acceptance.
                          It was this:
Approaching knowledge through analysis
constructed on the solid rock of fact,
and reared by logic, cautious and exact,
was fine in theory; but if atheists
were not thereby convinced that God exists,
then Reason wouldn't serve our purpose when
we hit the trail in search of God again.
The godless tribes encountered by our band
must be approached in terms they'd understand;
and only violence—brutal, blunt and blind—
impresses an agnostic's narrow mind.

   A thousand years went by before we'd dare
to venture onward. While we waited there
deliberately toughening our feet
against the desert's rocks and scorching heat,
a famous prophet in our midst arose.

The Apes of Eden: The Age of Thinkers

He beat his chest and howled, then blew his nose
and scratched an itch, and, climbing up a tree,
addressed the Tribe's assembled company:

"We've traveled far. We've searched the world around.
No nobler race than ours has yet been found.
It's clear that our corporeal design
must represent on Earth the Form Divine.
We apes have been Creation's final goal,
and thus endowed with Conscious Mind, and Soul."

We loudly cheered the prophet's words, as he
unveiled the product of his artistry.
It was an idol, standing two apes high
which showed—to viewers of discerning eye—
a perfect likeness of the artist, that
was twice his · height, and maybe thrice as fat.
The stoutness was for structural strength. This shape
was made of sunbaked earth from foot to nape.
The head was carved of wood, the teeth of bone.
Its painted eyes with canny wisdom shone.

Our prophet cried, "From this it's plain to see
our Quest is ended! God looks just like me!"
This doctrine, naturally, had some appeal
for those who liked "abstractions" they could feel,
and didn't care what those abstractions were;
but some of us, who felt he was too sure
of his unearthly handsomeness (and ours)
just left the converts building temple towers,
and moved to that oasis' farmost trees,
avoiding self-elected deities.

A mishap brought the idol to disgrace.
Some student priests, assigned to wash its face,
upset a bucket, and, as things evolved,
just watched in horror while their god dissolved.
Our prophet wasn't fazed. He sought our aid
rebuilding on the sludge of what he'd made.

Cried he, "Whoever dares to criticize,
let him succeed at everything he tries
—first crack, without experiment or skill.
Let those malign God's Messenger who will;
but let their prior records bear no shade
of failure, or success of second grade!
Speak up ! Where is the genius who can say
 he's never failed or erred in any way?
....So, if my god of clay was not too good,
I'll build a tougher one—of stone or wood!"

    He gained disciples, half the Tribe or more;
but not as many as he'd had before.
Just as the idol had resembled him,
so had the doctrines been the builder's whim,
and some whose god had needed to be changed
thought doctrines also should be rearranged.
From this we learned a "second try" results
in quite a new variety of cults.
The True Believers now decided they
were also qualified to work in clay.

THE DELUGE

Right here, I think, would be a likely place
to squeeze in one old myth which I'd erase
completely, were it wholly up to me,
from our accumulated history.
My view of myths is rather dim of course,
but some must be preserved, almost perforce.
Such tales are valued by the scribe who delves
for Symbols, though they're useless in themselves.

    Our senior tribesmen love to tell the tale
of how some humans in an ark, set sail
upon a fearful flood that drowned the world.
Above the highest hills the waters swirled,
while Fountains of the Deep profusely leaked,
and Heaven's windows on their hinges creaked.
If asked why heroes in their tale are men
instead of apes, the storytellers then
proceed to stuff your question down your throat:
they ask when apes have ever sailed a boat!
They have to tell the myth that way, because
they cannot change it—that's the way it was.

    You've read a number of my diatribes
about the gullibility of scribes,
who could have made things easier for me
by segregating myth from history.
I hesitate to bore my reader with
another long harangue on baseless myth.
Suffice it to be sure you understand
this Flood is here by popular demand,
and not because, I think the story's true.

I'm not the first to hold this point of view.
Some noted writers of antiquity
expressed the same opinion, pointedly.
Imagination is the only source
of any global Deluges, of course—
this world would be a better place to be
if there were water in such quantity.
But though they clearly gushed from gaffers first,
the Floods have spread, till my (more sober) thirst
for drier facts, compels me to imbibe
the same old Floods, recounted by a scribe!
We scribes should use our brains, as well as ears—
one can't make history of all one hears!

Though several versions of the tale exist,
the bulk of them are easy to resist.
One story stoutly claims that all around
the world, a mere three-tenths remained dry ground.
The other seven tenths of Earth, it's said
was swamped by "oceans" well above one's head.
[With Eden situated on a flat,
one asks, Would God have tolerated that?]
One scribe naively offers to relate
the Flood as fact, and even gives a date—
it seems the Deluge struck about the year
our idol-makers started to appear.

Am I somewhat less credulous than he,
or do I lack his "sense of history"?
I can't in Perfect Certitude rejoice,
and so I'll let my reader take his choice.

That year there was unprecedented rain,
which drenched the flat and had no place to drain.
It rained and rained, for forty days or more.
The plain became a fast-advancing shore
that rushed upon us at a mile a day.

It seemed a little dangerous to stay.

54 ♦ The Apes of Eden: The Age of Thinkers

But scouts, who went to search for higher ground,
reported that there were no hills around,
and hopes of reaching distant heights were slim
because, by then, we would have had to swim.
Already there was water all around;
our settlement was wholly "ocean" bound.
As our oasis kept on growing thin,
all we could do was watch the Flood pour in.

    At last all land was swamped. We sought the trees.
The rising, rushing water reached our knees,
then up to waist and shoulder, neck and head,
and swept away our still-protesting dead ....

    Since drought was absolute, until that year.
we couldn't understand such weather, here.
There's been some speculation, since that time,
that Powers That Were considered it a crime
of blasphemous proportions, building gods
of stuff as soluble as earthen clods,
and that whatever Power felt offended
thought it time all life on Earth was ended.

    That seems overdrawn, at least to me;
since we survived by climbing up a tree.
For history's sake, when all is said and done,
I wouldn't rob the gaffers of their fun.
This version's moral's easy to accept,
and that's the reason it's the one I've kept.
Historical details are none too plain
about the length of that peculiar rain,
to just what height the mountains flooded out,
the numbers drowned, or what it was about.
Results of it, regardless of its cause,
should be to give eccentric prophets pause:
The shivering survivors of the Flood
found all their gods and temples turned to mud.

    With Deluge written up, and conscience free

I'll now get back to sober history—
regretting that the Age I'm dealing with
right now, is not much soberer than myth.

THE REFORMATION

Succeeding prophets added further thoughts
on sacramental musts and shoulds and oughts;
on whether God had three—or just one—head;
and where an ape would go when he was dead.
(The pious were rewarded, by and by,
with peaches and bananas in the sky.)
They made up histories of gods and saints,
and gave us lists of sacred ams and aints,
describing God's intentions, aims and goals,
and things we'd have to do to save our souls—
or else get dunked in fiery lakes (glub, glub)
by chuckling minions of Beëlzebub.
They said which fables to believe were true
and which were spiritually good for you;
which books were God's transmitted honestly,
and which were merely pious forgery.
Because they had a Testimony strong
they had the Answers, and could not be wrong.
They knew, without the aid of Reason's light,
nor even learning how to read and write.

    Creation's defects were again explained.
Old Scratch had played his part, the proph's maintained.
While God Himself created what was best
(like apes, and ripe bananas) all the rest
was due to meddling by that Other Slob,
who made things tough for everyone. His job
was "testing" us with concrete evidence
to see if Faith was swayed by Common Sense.
Sound evidence for Truth would spoil us all,

and into careless habits we would fall;
but Faith, if tested thoroughly and long
with seeming contradictions, waxes strong.
The defects of creation seem to prove
that God does not exist. They thus remove
temptation to rely on Thought alone
and help us use our mental Twilight Zone.

    But Thought, which served us well through thin and thick,
was not a habit every ape could kick.
Forbidding us our curiosity
aroused instinctive animosity
and opened new horizons for disputes
on God, His Nature, and His Attributes.

    One God created apes. The god that's bad
then tested us to see what Faith we had.
He'd make us doubt our prophets, if he could.
Now surely such a scoundrel can't be good;
yet he's created by the Real God;
his no-Good schemes received the Goodly nod.
The Good God made good things. The Evil lout
then checked to see how well they tested out.
But when things failed, why weren't they then replaced
with Better things, so God was not disgraced
and His devout believers not annoyed
by all the Evil things this world enjoyed?

    Besides, if one God's kind, the other cruel,
the Two of Them should simply have a duel
God could settle Satan's hash for good
then run the cosmos as a Good God should.
And yet He'd never done this; He preferred
to tolerate the Devil.   This fact blurred
the sharp distinction prophets drew between
the God That's kindly and the one that's mean.
Backsliding hardheads claimed they couldn't tell
which god was God of Heaven, which of Hell.

Which prophet should a trusting layman heed,
when those who shared God's council disagreed
and every theologic tack they took
could be established by some tribal book?
When some outstanding prophet made his fame
among the masses, twenty more would claim
he was the tool of devil, spook or elf,
or made his revelations up himself
When thinkers disagreed, they cited rules
of logic broken by their rivals' schools.
When prophets clashed opinion, they would smirch
each others' factions as "the Devil's Church"—
thereby admitting that the Devil finds
a way to tamper with our prophets' minds.
What reassurance could a layman take
from revelations Lucifer could fake?
It left us only Faith, by which to choose
which sect was true, and which the Devil's ruse
to lure us to apostasy and sin.
Whichever choice one made, it "tied right in"
with what our Scriptures said—with just a few
corrections, with the scissors and the glue.

   Some tribesmen wondered, what should we infer
from defects in a prophet's character?
With ready access to the Godly Word,
you'd think he'd be serene and self-assured;
since apes who know their information's true
are less upset by other points of view
than those who feel a little insecure,
and have to compensate by acting sure.
A prophet was as peaceful as a dove,
and preached of mercy, meekness, joy and love,
until some clowning heckler raised a squawk—
then suddenly the dove became a hawk
and Retribution was the current theme.
The blistering invectives made it seem

that we could see the blazing brimstone fly.
We'd watch for lightning from a cloudless sky.

   There's nothing wrong with Righteous Wrath, of course
Eschewing logic's cool, persuasive force
a prophet couldn't reason with a clown;
the only thing to do was shout him down.
That shook our faith a little was the case
of prophets who had fallen to disgrace
(when caught, for instance, in a flagrant lie)
and rival churches raised the hue and cry
against impostor saints and all their sort.
You'd think he'd lose some popular support,
particularly when a saint was caught
defying creeds which he himself had taught.

   This rarely followed. When the cards were down,
exposure never tarnished his renown;
for even when his congregation learned
their saint was filching all the gold they earned,
it never did occur to anyone
to question creeds the prophet had begun.
That someone was a liar and a thief
And prophet too, inspired no disbelief.
His teachings, and the trust he had abused,
were separate matters, not to be confused.
A scoundrel, yes; and charlatan, and clod—
but when he prophesied, he spoke for God.

   We had a difficult theology,
but that would also test our Faith, you see.
Though philosophic puzzles might evolve,
these, too, were problems stubborn Faith would solve.

   It finally did. When things got out of hand,
we had a Reformation in the land.
In this, the motivator of it all
was one old Chief with something on the ball.
He made no inspirational pretense.

He was no prophet, just an ape with sense.

   "Look, fellows; things have gone from bad to worse,"
he told us. "Revelations are a curse;
they're not the blessing that the prophets say.
Religion hasn't always been this way.
As soon as tribal prophets learn to hear
what God is saying, useless creeds appear
and Eden's Tribe splits up in squabbling sects
that neither argument nor God corrects.
We used to know far less, but had a creed
—or lack of one—on which we all agreed.

   "You'd think if truth revealed by God is true,
His prophets would at least say something new;
and yet in search of God they've come no nearer
than they'd get by gazing in a mirror.
Apes are wise. Agreed? So God is, too.
What might He look like? Just like me or you!
The Tribe is great, and so is God, they say.
We're wonderful, so He must be that way.
We love to wrangle over creeds and all,
so God jumped in to join our verbal brawl.
We've made a narcissistic verbal wad
of virtues we admire, and called it 'God.'
You'd think that even dopes like us should see
this isn't how to learn theology.
What trash to found belief in God upon!
'Great Ape' is what we'll call Him, from now on!
We all hate snakes—and naturally assume
that God Himself would give one lots of room;
they are the Devil's work. Who told us so?
God takes the things to bed, for all we know!
If snakes had prophets, would their god not be
elongate, sinuous and slippery?
   "Our forebears took the Cyclopes for gods—
and later learned they were ungodly clods.
Must we repeat, through all these centuries,

the same mistakes, by prophets such as these?
I don't know what God's like; but this I'll say:
He won't resemble them in any way!
Moreover, frankly, fellows , in my view,
the Attributes of God can't be too few.
The more we try to pin the Concept down,
the more it turns from gold to apish brown.
There's one more thing I know: God isn't here
in this oasis. Every passing year
we spend in hearing prophets eloquate
is one more year our real Quest must wait!"

   The Chief raved on, his temper in a froth,
until his tirade roused us from our sloth.
The wisest thing our Tribe had ever done
was martyr all our prophets, one by one.
We stormed the temples in our righteous wrath
and left a trail of carnage in our path.

THE MYSTICS

When disillusionment was nearly ripe,
another saint, a less pretentious type,
invited us to lend our tribal ear
and launched upon his honest, brief career:

    "Admitting that the world's ineptly made,
I don't believe we came out short to trade
the Garden's easy but myopic scope
for broader views, and more ambitious hope,
and more to think about and more to do—
but this is where I can't agree with you:
You say you think the Ultimately Good
can still be found by searching. If it could
then wouldn't we have found It long ago?
A million years we searched, through sun and snow,
through forest depths, across the treeless plain,
through parching drought and then through flood and rain.
The natives mock us, everywhere we go—
but could it be there's something we don't know?
Might they have found, by staying in one place,
some Secret which eludes a roving race?
Our tribal Quest I never would deride,
but surely none can say we haven't tried!
A million years we've sought the Good and True
with no results—so let's try something new.
The doctrine of our Godly pulchritude
was flattering at first, but much too crude.
One aspect of that theory, though, is sound
our minds are nearly perfect, all around,
and therefore must by nature manifest

some aspect of the Object of our Quest.
My plan is this: Let's see if we can find
divine reflections in the Conscious Mind.
Such research won't be finished in a year,
nor yet in several centuries; but here
in this grim desert which we call our own
we've time to spare—at least we're left alone.
The country's stark enough no foe will strive
to wrest it from us; yet we can survive,
perhaps to learn, when we've had time to think,
we've lived for years upon the Secret's brink."

 We never did find out what might result
had he remained alive, to guide his cult.
His doctrine, less fantastic than the rest,
impressed a lot of us, among the best.
He ran afoul of anti-prophet verve
and met a fate he didn't quite deserve.

 The founder was himself a mystic; but
his place was taken by a real nut!
The second leader of the movement taught
the world consists of manifested thought
—a sort of Universal Dream—which he
could teach us to intuit, mystically.
The Guru taught his students how to spy
new Realms of Being, through the Inner Eye.
Assuming postures like a figure eight
which nonbelievers can't approximate,
they'd leave this shadow world, corrupt and crude,
to visit planes of Sheer Beatitude
for brief Reunion with Eternity,
like drops of rain returning to the sea.

 What sights they saw, in meditative trance!
where mystic visions, fraught with Meaning, dance—
resplendent insights into Higher Realms,
where Union with the Cosmos overwhelms

the fears and doubts that plague the earthbound soul
who lacks the mystic's Inner-Self control!
What sempiternal music bathed their ears—
the haunting harmonies of whirling Spheres!

    They manifested aptitudes occult
and unexampled, as a first result.
They knew where stolen objects must be sought.
They read our minds, divining every thought,
and told us everything we'd ever done.
They lifted weights of better than a ton
attached to ropes they held between their teeth.
They sat on air, with nothing underneath.
They'd teleport themselves from place to place,
not passing through the intervening space.

    Not knowing what to think, we asked our Chief.
The verdict he returned was blunt and brief:

    "The answers these fanatics say they find
are self-delusions from a fevered mind.
You'd get the same results by chewing weeds,
inhaling fumes, or munching cactus seeds.
A God exists, somewhere; but what He is
we'll never learn by mystic psycho-quiz
of multistoried minds. We must go see
before we'll know if God's an 'It' or 'He'."

    The Guru was a threat. In days of yore
we lacked the guts we're now so famous for.
We couldn't comprehend that mystic crew,
but time went on, and still their numbers grew.
Their method was becoming quite a craze,
and we had lost all patience with delays;
so, lest his gulls perpetuate his lie,
we strung him up, and let his teachings die.

    Yet some time later, when we felt prepared
for travels which before we hadn't dared,

we found the mystics very much extant.
That heresy was hard to kill, I'll grant.
The Guru's followers explained that he,
though dead, was greater than mortality.
Although the author of their creed was gone,
his words and thoughts—and hence his mind—lived on.
By this semantic dodge, they made it seem
that killing them would help to prove their theme.

   The error of their views was evident.
Our wisest, unimpressed, picked up and went.
The issue was as clear as day and night:
the Guru's bunch was wrong, and we were right.
But when the Tribe set out across the plain,
three quarters of us opted to remain.

   The Prophet Era, though, was finally through.
The Remnant of the Tribe set forth anew
to seek the Logos, once theology
had strangled in its own apology.
We didn't take the course the human race
had blundered into. This was not a case
of Thesis clashing with Antithesis,
resulting in misleading Synthesis;
we simply purged the pithecanic mind
of sterile thought, and left all that behind.
And if the scribes retained some small percent
of our mistake, it was by accident.

   For God cannot be carved from rock or log,
nor molded from a cloud of verbal fog,
nor glimpsed in dazzling visions you obtain
by shorting out the circuits in your brain.
Our theologues were wrong to speculate.
We're glad we had that Chief to set us straight.
For sound conceits of God, we've him to thank:
a formless Absolute,
a Sacred Blank.

ABOUT THE AUTHOR

Jon P. Gunn wrote *The Apes of Eden Saga* over a period of many, many years. He read Spenser, Chaucer, Dante and Cervantes. He died while still intermittently adding chapters. Many oddball philosophies, from solopsism to deism are explored and mocked. Allusions to a broad spectrum of myths and canons are made.

Jon never graduated from college even though he had twice the number of hours to graduate. He was too busy reading the great works of literature to bother. He shared the Apes of Eden with a good friend. It is that man and his friend, Rick Lakin who are bringing you Jon's work. We think it's very good. We hope you do too.